P9-BZV-388

Amish

Country
Cookbook

pi

Publications International, Ltd.

Copyright © 2008 Publications International, Ltd.
All rights reserved. This publication may not be reproduced or quoted in whole or in part by any means whatsoever without written permission from:

Louis Weber, CEO
Publications International, Ltd.
7373 North Cicero Avenue
Lincolnwood, Illinois 60712

Permission is never granted for commercial purposes.

Some of the products listed in this publication may be in limited distribution.

Cover illustrated by Robert Crawford.

Interior Illustrations by Roberta Polfus.

ISBN-13: 978-1-4127-7127-6
ISBN-10: 1-4127-7127-7

Manufactured in China.

8 7 6 5 4 3 2 1

Microwave Cooking: Microwave ovens vary in wattage. Use the cooking times as guidelines and check for doneness before adding more time.

Preparation/Cooking Times: Preparation times are based on the approximate amount of time required to assemble the recipe before cooking, baking, chilling or serving. These times include preparation steps such as measuring, chopping and mixing. The fact that some preparations and cooking can be done simultaneously is taken into account. Preparation of optional ingredients and serving suggestions is not included.

CONTENTS

SIMPLE GOODNESS

The Amish live a simple and unpretentious life, and that is reflected in their cooking. Their meals are made from scratch, using fresh or canned ingredients that were grown mostly in their gardens and produced on their farms.

Hearty and homemade, Amish meals are considered the epitome of comfort food. Among the mainstays are mashed potatoes with gravy, chicken potpie, brisket with noodles, meatloaf, and buttermilk biscuits—foods that are deeply satisfying and delicious. And don't forget dessert: Apple-buttermilk pie and berry cobbler are traditional and well-loved meal-ending treats!

The recipes inside *Amish Country Cookbook* are wholesome—and they're easy to prepare! You'll be delighted to discover that making authentic Amish food is simple—just like the Amish lifestyle.

MAIN DISHES

Baked Barbecue Chicken

1 cut-up whole chicken (about 3 pounds)
1 small onion, cut into slices
1 1/2 cups ketchup
1/2 cup packed light brown sugar
1/4 cup Worcestershire sauce
2 tablespoons lemon juice
1 tablespoon liquid smoke

1. Preheat oven to 375°F. Spray 13×9-inch baking dish with nonstick cooking spray. Place chicken in prepared dish; top with onion slices.

2. Combine ketchup, brown sugar, Worcestershire sauce, lemon juice and liquid smoke in small saucepan. Cook and stir over medium heat 2 to 3 minutes or until sugar dissolves. Pour over chicken.

3. Bake 1 hour or until chicken is cooked through (165°F). Discard onion slices. Let stand 10 minutes before serving. *Makes 6 servings*

Serving Suggestion: *Serve with baked potatoes, crusty French bread and tossed green salad.*

Beef Stroganoff Casserole

1 pound ground beef
1 teaspoon vegetable oil
8 ounces sliced mushrooms
1 large onion, chopped
3 cloves garlic, minced
$^1/_4$ cup dry white wine
1 can (10$^3/_4$ ounces) condensed cream of mushroom soup,
    undiluted
$^1/_2$ cup sour cream
1 tablespoon Dijon mustard
$^1/_4$ teaspoon salt
$^1/_8$ teaspoon black pepper
4 cups cooked egg noodles
    Chopped fresh parsley (optional)

1. Preheat oven to 350°F. Spray 13×9-inch baking dish with nonstick cooking spray.

2. Brown beef in large skillet over medium-high heat 6 minutes until no longer pink, stirring to break up meat. Drain fat. Remove beef from skillet and set aside.

3. Heat oil in same skillet over medium-high heat. Add mushrooms, onion and garlic; cook and stir 2 minutes or until onion is tender. Add wine. Reduce heat to medium-low and simmer 3 minutes. Remove from heat; stir in soup, sour cream, mustard, salt and pepper until well blended. Return beef to skillet; stir to blend.

4. Place noodles in prepared dish. Pour beef mixture over noodles; stir until noodles are well coated. Bake, uncovered, 30 minutes or until heated through. Sprinkle with parsley.   *Makes 6 servings*

Buttermilk Oven-Fried Chicken

1¹/₂ cups buttermilk
1 tablespoon plus 1 teaspoon garlic powder, divided
2 teaspoons salt
2 teaspoons dried thyme, divided
1 teaspoon dried sage
1 teaspoon paprika
¹/₂ teaspoon black pepper
2¹/₂ pounds chicken pieces, skin removed
*   Nonstick cooking spray*
1¹/₂ cups panko bread crumbs*
¹/₄ cup all-purpose flour

*Panko bread crumbs are light, crispy, Japanese-style bread crumbs. They can be found in the Asian aisle of most supermarkets. Unseasoned dry bread crumbs can be substituted.

1. Whisk buttermilk, 1 tablespoon garlic powder, salt, 1 teaspoon thyme, sage, paprika and pepper in large bowl until well blended. Add chicken; turn to coat. Cover and refrigerate at least 5 hours or overnight.

2. Preheat oven to 400°F. Line 2 baking sheets with foil; spray with cooking spray. Set aside.

3. Combine bread crumbs, flour, remaining 1 teaspoon garlic powder and 1 teaspoon thyme in large shallow bowl. Remove chicken from buttermilk mixture, allowing excess to drip off. Coat chicken pieces one at a time with crumb mixture. Shake off excess crumbs. Place on prepared baking sheets; let stand 10 minutes.

4. Spray tops of chicken pieces with cooking spray. Bake about 50 minutes or until golden brown and chicken is cooked through (165°F), turning once and spraying with additional cooking spray halfway through baking time.

Makes about 8 servings

Chicken Divan Casserole

1 cup uncooked rice
1 cup coarsely shredded carrots
  Nonstick cooking spray
4 boneless skinless chicken breasts
2 tablespoons butter
3 tablespoons all-purpose flour
1/4 teaspoon salt
  Black pepper
1 cup chicken broth
1/2 cup milk or half-and-half
1/4 cup dry white wine
1/3 cup plus 2 tablespoons grated Parmesan cheese, divided
1 pound frozen broccoli florets

1. Preheat oven to 350°F. Lightly grease 12×8-inch baking dish.

2. Prepare rice according to package directions. Stir in carrots. Spread mixture into prepared baking dish.

3. Spray large skillet with cooking spray. Heat over medium-high heat. Brown chicken breasts 2 minutes on each side. Arrange over rice.

4. To prepare sauce, melt butter in 2-quart saucepan over medium heat. Whisk in flour, salt and pepper to taste; cook and stir 1 minute. Gradually whisk in broth and milk. Cook and stir until mixture comes to a boil. Reduce heat; simmer 2 minutes. Stir in wine. Remove from heat. Stir in 1/3 cup cheese.

5. Arrange broccoli around chicken. Pour sauce over top. Sprinkle remaining 2 tablespoons cheese over chicken.

6. Cover with foil; bake 30 minutes. Remove foil; bake 10 to 15 minutes or until chicken is no longer pink in center and broccoli is hot.

Makes 6 servings

Chicken, Asparagus & Mushroom Bake

1 tablespoon butter
1 tablespoon olive oil
2 boneless skinless chicken breasts (about $^1/_2$ pound), cut into
    bite-size pieces
2 cloves garlic, minced
1 cup sliced mushrooms
2 cups sliced asparagus
    Black pepper
1 package (about 6 ounces) corn bread stuffing mix
$^1/_4$ cup dry white wine (optional)
1 can (about 14 ounces) reduced-sodium chicken broth
1 can ($10^3/_4$ ounces) condensed cream of asparagus or cream of
    chicken soup, undiluted

1. Preheat oven to 350°F. Heat butter and oil in large skillet until butter is melted. Add chicken and garlic; cook and stir about 3 minutes over medium-high heat until chicken is cooked through. Add mushrooms; cook and stir 2 minutes. Add asparagus; cook and stir about 5 minutes or until asparagus is crisp-tender. Season with pepper.

2. Transfer mixture to $2^1/_2$-quart casserole or 6 small casseroles. Top with stuffing mix.

3. Add wine to skillet, if desired; cook and stir 1 minute over medium-high heat, scraping up any browned bits from bottom of skillet. Add broth and soup; cook and stir until well blended.

4. Pour broth mixture over stuffing mix; mix well. Bake, uncovered, about 35 minutes (30 minutes for small casseroles) or until heated through and lightly browned.   *Makes 6 servings*

Note: This is a good way to stretch a little leftover chicken into an easy and tasty dinner.

Family-Style Creamy Chicken and Noodles

    8 ounces uncooked wide egg noodles
    4 cups water
    1 pound boneless skinless chicken breasts
1 1/2 cups chopped onions
  3/4 cup chopped celery
  1/2 teaspoon salt
  1/2 teaspoon dried thyme
    1 bay leaf
  1/8 teaspoon white pepper
    1 can (10 3/4 ounces) condensed cream of chicken soup, undiluted
  1/2 cup buttermilk
    Chopped fresh parsley (optional)

1. Cook pasta according to package directions; drain. Set aside.

2. Meanwhile, bring water to a boil in Dutch oven over high heat. Add chicken breasts, onions, celery, salt, thyme, bay leaf and white pepper. Return to a boil. Reduce heat to low; simmer, uncovered, 35 minutes until chicken is no longer pink in center. Remove chicken; cut into 1/2-inch pieces. Set aside.

3. Increase heat to high. Return liquid in Dutch oven to a boil. Continue cooking until liquid and vegetables have reduced to 1 cup. Remove from heat; discard bay leaf. Whisk in soup and buttermilk until well blended. Add chicken pieces and pasta; toss to blend. Garnish with parsley.

Makes 6 servings

Ham with Apple Cherry Sauce

1 (3-pound) canned ham
$^3/_4$ cup apple juice, divided
2 tablespoons cornstarch
1 cup chopped apples
$^1/_2$ cup cherry or currant jelly

1. Bake ham according to package directions. Combine $^1/_4$ cup apple juice and cornstarch in small bowl; stir until smooth. Set aside.

2. Place apples, jelly and remaining $^1/_2$ cup apple juice in large saucepan. Heat over medium-high heat. Cook 5 minutes. Add cornstarch mixture; cook and stir 1 minute until thickened.

3. Slice ham. Serve with sauce.   *Makes 8 to 10 servings*

Roast Chicken with Peppers

1 cut-up whole chicken (3 to $3^1/_2$ pounds)
3 tablespoons olive oil, divided
1 tablespoon plus $1^1/_2$ teaspoons chopped fresh rosemary leaves
    or $1^1/_2$ teaspoons dried rosemary
1 tablespoon fresh lemon juice
$1^1/_4$ teaspoons salt, divided
$^3/_4$ teaspoon black pepper, divided
3 bell peppers (preferably 1 red, 1 yellow and 1 green)
1 medium onion

1. Preheat oven to 375°F. Place chicken in shallow roasting pan.

2. Combine 2 tablespoons oil, rosemary and lemon juice; brush over chicken. Sprinkle 1 teaspoon salt and $^1/_2$ teaspoon pepper over chicken. Roast 15 minutes.

3. Cut bell peppers lengthwise into $^1/_2$-inch-thick strips. Cut onion into thin wedges. Toss vegetables with remaining 1 tablespoon oil, $^1/_4$ teaspoon salt and $^1/_4$ teaspoon pepper. Spoon vegetables around chicken; roast about 40 minutes or until vegetables are tender and chicken is cooked through (165°F). Serve chicken with vegetables and pan juices.   *Makes 6 servings*

Homestyle Skillet Chicken

1 tablespoon Cajun seasoning
$\frac{1}{2}$ teaspoon plus $\frac{1}{8}$ teaspoon black pepper, divided
$\frac{1}{2}$ teaspoon salt, divided
8 chicken thighs
2 tablespoons vegetable oil
4 cloves garlic, minced
8 small red or new potatoes, quartered
12 pearl onions, peeled*
1 cup baby carrots
2 stalks celery, halved lengthwise and sliced diagonally into
  $\frac{1}{2}$-inch pieces
$\frac{1}{2}$ red bell pepper, diced
2 tablespoons all-purpose flour
1 cup reduced-sodium chicken broth
$\frac{1}{2}$ cup sherry
2 tablespoons finely chopped fresh parsley

*To peel pearl onions, drop into boiling water for 30 seconds, then plunge immediately into ice water. The peel should slide right off.

1. Combine Cajun seasoning, $\frac{1}{2}$ teaspoon black pepper and $\frac{1}{4}$ teaspoon salt in small bowl. Rub mixture onto all sides of chicken.

2. Heat oil in large heavy skillet over medium-high heat. Add garlic and chicken; cook until chicken is browned, about 3 minutes per side. Transfer chicken to plate; set aside.

3. Add potatoes, onions, carrots, celery and bell pepper to skillet; cook and stir 3 minutes. Sprinkle flour over vegetables; stir to coat. Slowly stir in chicken broth and sherry, scraping up browned bits from bottom of skillet. Bring mixture to a boil, stirring constantly.

4. Reduce heat to medium-low. Return chicken to skillet. Cover and cook about 30 minutes or until chicken is cooked through (165°F). Increase heat to medium-high; cook, uncovered, about 5 minutes or until sauce is thickened.

5. Season with remaining $\frac{1}{4}$ teaspoon salt and $\frac{1}{8}$ teaspoon black pepper. Sprinkle with parsley.

Makes 4 servings

Italian-Style Brisket

$^3/_4$ cup fat-free reduced-sodium beef broth, divided
$^1/_2$ cup chopped onion
  1 clove garlic, minced
  1 can (about 14 ounces) diced tomatoes
$^1/_4$ cup dry red wine
$^3/_4$ teaspoon dried oregano
$^1/_4$ teaspoon dried thyme
$^1/_4$ teaspoon black pepper
  1 small well-trimmed beef brisket (about 1$^1/_4$ pounds)
  3 cups sliced mushrooms
  3 cups halved (lengthwise) and thinly sliced zucchini
     (about 1 pound)
  3 cups cooked wide egg noodles

1. Heat $^1/_4$ cup beef broth in Dutch oven. Add onion and garlic; cover and simmer 5 minutes.

2. Stir in tomatoes, remaining $^1/_2$ cup beef broth, red wine, oregano, thyme and pepper. Bring to a boil. Reduce heat to low; add beef brisket. Cover; simmer 1$^1/_2$ hours, basting occasionally with tomato mixture.

3. Add mushrooms and zucchini; cover and simmer 30 to 45 minutes or until beef is tender.

4. Remove beef. Simmer vegetable mixture 5 to 10 minutes to thicken slightly. Cut beef across the grain into 12 thin slices. Serve beef with vegetable sauce and noodles.   *Makes 6 servings*

Kielbasa and Sauerkraut Skillet Dinner

2 tablespoons olive oil
1 pound kielbasa sausage, cut into $1/4$-inch-thick slices
1 small red onion, thinly sliced
1 small green bell pepper, cored, seeded and thinly sliced
2 cups sauerkraut, rinsed and well drained
2 teaspoons Dijon mustard
$1/2$ teaspoon caraway seeds
$1/4$ teaspoon salt
$1/4$ teaspoon black pepper

1. Heat oil in large skillet. Add sausage, onion and bell pepper. Cook over medium heat 5 to 10 minutes or until vegetables are tender and sausage is lightly browned, stirring occasionally. Drain fat.

2. Add sauerkraut, mustard, caraway seeds, salt and black pepper to skillet. Cook over medium heat 3 to 5 minutes or until heated through.

Makes 4 servings

Maple-Mustard Pork Chops

2 tablespoons maple syrup
1 tablespoon olive oil
2 teaspoons whole-grain mustard
2 center-cut pork loin chops (6 ounces each)
Nonstick cooking spray
$1/3$ cup water

1. Preheat oven to 375°F. Combine maple syrup, olive oil and mustard in small bowl. Brush syrup mixture over both sides of pork chops.

2. Spray medium ovenproof skillet with cooking spray; heat over medium-high heat. Add chops; brown on both sides. Add water; cover and bake 20 to 30 minutes or until barely pink in centers. *Makes 2 servings*

Potato-Sausage Casserole

1 pound bulk pork sausage or ground pork
1 can (10 ¾ ounces) condensed cream of mushroom soup,
   undiluted
¾ cup milk
½ cup chopped onion
½ teaspoon salt
¼ teaspoon black pepper
3 cups sliced potatoes
½ tablespoon butter, cut into small pieces
1½ cups (6 ounces) shredded Cheddar cheese

1. *Preheat oven to 350°F. Spray 1½-quart casserole with nonstick cooking spray; set aside.*

2. *Brown sausage in large skillet over medium heat 6 minutes, stirring to break up meat; drain fat.*

3. *Stir together soup, milk, onion, salt and pepper in medium bowl.*

4. *Place half of potatoes in prepared casserole. Top with half of soup mixture; top with half of sausage. Repeat layers, ending with sausage. Dot with butter.*

5. *Cover casserole with foil. Bake 1¼ to 1½ hours or until potatoes are tender. Uncover; sprinkle with cheese. Return to oven; bake until cheese is melted and casserole is bubbly.*   *Makes 6 servings*

Southern Fried Catfish with Hush Puppies

Hush Puppy Batter (page 36)
4 catfish fillets (about 1¹/₂ pounds)
¹/₂ cup yellow cornmeal
3 tablespoons all-purpose flour
1¹/₂ teaspoons salt
¹/₄ teaspoon ground red pepper
Vegetable oil

1. *Prepare Hush Puppy Batter; set aside.*

2. *Rinse catfish; pat dry with paper towels. Combine cornmeal, flour, salt and red pepper in shallow dish. Dip fish into cornmeal mixture. Heat 1 inch oil in large heavy skillet over medium heat until 375°F on deep-fry thermometer.*

3. *Cook fish in batches 4 to 5 minutes or until golden brown and fish begins to flake when tested with fork. Allow temperature of oil to return to 375°F between batches. Drain fish on paper towels.*

4. *To make Hush Puppies, drop batter by tablespoonfuls into hot oil. Cook in batches 2 minutes or until golden brown. Drain on paper towels.*

Makes 4 servings

Spicy Chicken Casserole with Corn Bread

2 tablespoons olive oil
4 boneless skinless chicken breasts, cut into bite-size pieces
1 package (about 1 ounce) taco seasoning mix
1 can (about 15 ounces) black beans, rinsed and drained
1 can (14 1/2 ounces) diced tomatoes, drained
1 can (about 10 ounces) Mexican-style corn, drained
1 can (about 4 ounces) diced mild green chiles, drained
1/2 cup mild salsa
1 box (about 8 1/2 ounces) corn bread mix, plus ingredients to prepare mix
1/2 cup (2 ounces) shredded Cheddar cheese
1/4 cup chopped red bell pepper

1. *Preheat oven to 350°F. Spray 2-quart casserole with nonstick cooking spray. Set aside. Heat oil in large skillet over medium heat. Cook chicken until cooked through.*

2. *Sprinkle taco seasoning over chicken. Add black beans, tomatoes, corn, chiles and salsa; stir until well blended. Transfer to prepared dish.*

3. *Prepare corn bread mix according to package directions, adding cheese and bell pepper. Spread batter over chicken mixture.*

4. *Bake 30 minutes or until corn bread is golden brown.*

Makes 4 to 6 servings

Spicy Pork Chop Casserole

Nonstick cooking spray
2 cups frozen corn
2 cups frozen diced hash brown potatoes
1 can (about 14 ounces) diced tomatoes with basil, garlic and
    oregano, drained
2 teaspoons chili powder
1 teaspoon dried oregano
$1/2$ teaspoon ground cumin
$1/8$ teaspoon red pepper flakes
1 teaspoon olive oil
4 boneless pork loin chops (about 3 ounces each),
    cut about $3/4$ inch thick
$1/4$ teaspoon black pepper
$1/4$ cup (1 ounce) shredded Monterey Jack cheese

1. Preheat oven to 375°F.

2. Lightly spray large nonstick skillet with cooking spray. Add corn; cook
and stir over medium-high heat about 5 minutes or until corn begins to
brown. Add potatoes; cook and stir about 5 minutes more or until potatoes
begin to brown. Add tomatoes, chili powder, oregano, cumin and red pepper
flakes; stir until blended.

3. Lightly spray 8×8-inch baking dish with cooking spray. Transfer corn
mixture to prepared dish.

4. Wipe skillet with paper towel. Add oil and pork chops to skillet. Cook
over medium-high heat until browned on one side. Place browned side up
on top of corn mixture in baking dish. Sprinkle with black pepper. Bake,
uncovered, 20 minutes or until meat is barely pink in center. Sprinkle with
cheese. Let stand 2 to 3 minutes before serving.

Makes 4 servings

Prep Time: 15 minutes
Bake Time: 20 minutes

SOUPS

Carrot Soup

2 teaspoons butter
$1/3$ cup chopped onion
1 tablespoon chopped fresh ginger
1 pound baby carrots
$1/2$ teaspoon salt
$1/4$ teaspoon black pepper
3 cups vegetable broth
$1/4$ cup whipping cream
$1/4$ cup orange juice
Pinch ground nutmeg
4 tablespoons sour cream

1. Melt butter in large saucepan over high heat. Add onion and ginger; cook and stir about 1 minute or until ginger is fragrant. Stir in carrots, salt and pepper; cook and stir 2 minutes.

2. Stir in broth; bring to a boil. Reduce heat to medium-low; cover and simmer 30 minutes or until carrots are tender.

3. Transfer soup to blender, half at a time; blend until smooth. Return to saucepan and stir in cream, orange juice and nutmeg; heat through. Thin soup with additional broth, if necessary. Top each serving with dollop of sour cream. *Makes 4 servings*

Corn and Tomato Chowder

1½ cups peeled and diced plum tomatoes
¾ teaspoon salt, divided
2 ears corn, husks removed
1 tablespoon butter
½ cup finely chopped shallots
1 clove garlic, minced
1 can (12 ounces) evaporated skimmed milk
1 cup chicken broth
1 tablespoon finely chopped fresh sage or 1 teaspoon rubbed sage
¼ teaspoon black pepper
1 tablespoon cornstarch
2 tablespoons cold water

1. Place tomatoes in nonmetal colander over bowl. Sprinkle with
½ teaspoon salt; toss to mix well. Allow tomatoes to drain at least 1 hour.

2. Meanwhile, cut corn kernels off cobs into small bowl. Scrape cobs with
dull side of knife to extract liquid from cobs into same bowl; set aside.
Discard 1 cob; break remaining cob in half.

3. Heat butter in heavy medium saucepan over medium-high heat until
melted and bubbly. Add shallots and garlic; reduce heat to low. Cover and
cook about 5 minutes or until shallots are soft and translucent. Add milk,
broth, sage, pepper and reserved corn cob halves. Bring to a boil over high
heat. Reduce heat to low; simmer, uncovered, 10 minutes. Remove and
discard cob halves.

4. Add corn with liquid; return to a boil over medium-high heat. Reduce
heat to low; simmer, uncovered, 15 minutes more. Dissolve cornstarch
in water; add to chowder. Stir until thickened. Remove from heat; stir
in drained tomatoes and remaining ¼ teaspoon salt. Spoon into bowls.
Garnish with additional fresh sage, if desired.   Makes 4 to 6 servings

Country Bean Soup

1¼ cups dried navy beans or lima beans, rinsed and drained
2½ cups water
¼ pound salt pork or fully cooked ham, chopped
¼ cup chopped onion
½ teaspoon dried oregano
¼ teaspoon salt
¼ teaspoon ground ginger
¼ teaspoon dried sage
¼ teaspoon black pepper
2 cups milk
2 tablespoons butter

1. Place navy beans in large saucepan; add enough water to cover beans. Bring to a boil; reduce heat and simmer 2 minutes. Remove from heat; cover and let stand for 1 hour. (Or, cover beans with water and soak overnight.)

2. Drain beans and return to saucepan. Stir in 2½ cups water, salt pork, onion, oregano, salt, ginger, sage and pepper. Bring to a boil; reduce heat. Cover and simmer 2 to 2½ hours or until beans are tender. (If necessary, add more water during cooking.) Add milk and butter; cook and stir until mixture is heated through and butter is melted. Season with additional salt and pepper, if desired. *Makes 6 servings*

Country Chicken Chowder

1 pound chicken tenders
2 tablespoons butter or margarine
1 small onion, chopped
1 stalk celery, sliced
1 small carrot, sliced
1 can (10¾ ounces) condensed cream of potato soup, undiluted
1 cup milk
1 cup frozen corn
½ teaspoon dried dill weed

1. Cut chicken tenders into ½-inch pieces.

2. Melt butter in large saucepan or Dutch oven over medium-high heat. Add chicken; cook and stir 5 minutes.

3. Add onion, celery and carrot; cook and stir 3 minutes. Stir in soup, milk, corn and dill; reduce heat to low. Cook about 8 minutes or until corn is tender and chowder is heated through. Add salt and pepper to taste.

Makes 4 servings

Tip: For a special touch, garnish soup with croutons and fresh dill. For a hearty winter meal, serve the chowder in hollowed-out toasted French rolls or small round sourdough loaves.

Prep and Cook Time: *27 minutes*

Ground Beef, Spinach and Barley Soup

12 ounces ground beef
4 cups water
1 can (about 14 ounces) stewed tomatoes
1½ cups thinly sliced carrots
1 cup chopped onion
½ cup quick-cooking barley
1½ teaspoons beef bouillon granules
1½ teaspoons dried thyme
1 teaspoon dried oregano
½ teaspoon garlic powder
¼ teaspoon black pepper
⅛ teaspoon salt
3 cups torn stemmed washed spinach leaves

1. Brown beef in large saucepan over medium heat 6 minutes until no longer pink, stirring to separate meat. Rinse beef under warm water; drain. Return beef to saucepan; add water, stewed tomatoes, carrots, onion, barley, bouillon granules, thyme, oregano, garlic powder, pepper and salt.

2. Bring to a boil over high heat. Reduce heat to medium-low. Cover and simmer 12 to 15 minutes or until barley and vegetables are tender, stirring occasionally. Stir in spinach; cook until spinach starts to wilt.

Makes 4 servings

Pork and Cabbage Soup

$^1/_2$ *pound pork loin, cut into* $^1/_2$*-inch cubes*
1 medium onion, chopped
2 strips bacon, finely chopped
2 cups canned beef broth
2 cups canned chicken broth
1 can (28 ounces) diced tomatoes, drained
2 medium carrots, sliced
$^3/_4$ *teaspoon dried marjoram*
1 bay leaf
$^1/_8$ *teaspoon black pepper*
$^1/_4$ *medium cabbage, chopped*
2 tablespoons chopped fresh parsley
Additional chopped fresh parsley

1. *Cook and stir pork, onion and bacon in 5-quart Dutch oven over medium heat until onion is slightly tender. Remove from heat. Drain fat.*

2. *Stir in beef broth and chicken broth. Stir in tomatoes, carrots, marjoram, bay leaf and pepper. Bring to a boil over high heat. Reduce heat to medium-low; simmer, uncovered, about 30 minutes. Remove and discard bay leaf. Skim off fat.*

3. *Stir cabbage into soup. Bring to a boil over high heat. Reduce heat to medium-low; simmer, uncovered, about 15 minutes or until cabbage is tender.*

4. *Remove soup from heat; stir in 2 tablespoons parsley. Ladle into bowls. Garnish each serving with additional parsley.*   *Makes 6 servings*

Rustic Country Turkey Soup

1 cup chopped onions
³/₄ cup sliced carrots
   Nonstick cooking spray
4 ounces sliced mushrooms
1 teaspoon minced garlic
2 cans (14 ounces) chicken broth
2 ounces uncooked, whole wheat rotini
1 teaspoon dried thyme or dried parsley
¹/₄ to ¹/₂ teaspoon poultry seasoning
¹/₈ teaspoon red pepper flakes
2 cups chopped, cooked turkey breast
2 tablespoons olive oil
¹/₄ cup chopped parsley
¹/₄ teaspoon salt

1. Place Dutch oven over medium-high heat until hot. Coat with cooking spray. Add onions and carrots. Spray vegetables with cooking spray. Cook and stir 2 minutes. Add mushrooms; cook 2 minutes more. Add garlic; cook and stir 30 seconds. Add broth. Bring to a boil.

2. Add rotini, thyme, poultry seasoning and pepper flakes. Bring back to a boil. Reduce heat. Cover; simmer 8 minutes or until pasta is tender.

3. Remove from heat. Add turkey, olive oil, parsley and salt. Cover. Let stand 5 minutes before serving.   *Makes 5 servings*

Smoky Navy Bean Soup

Nonstick cooking spray
4 ounces Canadian bacon or extra-lean ham, diced
1 cup diced onions
1 large carrot, thinly sliced
1 stalk celery, thinly sliced
3 cups water
6 ounces red potatoes, diced
2 bay leaves
1/4 teaspoon dried tarragon
1 can (15 ounces) navy beans, rinsed and drained
1 1/2 tablespoons olive oil
1 1/2 teaspoons liquid smoke
1/2 teaspoon salt (optional)
1/2 teaspoon black pepper

1. *Heat Dutch oven over medium-high heat; spray with cooking spray. Add bacon or ham; cook 2 minutes until brown. Transfer to plate.*

2. *Add onions, carrot and celery to Dutch oven; spray with cooking spray. Cook and stir 4 minutes or until onions are translucent. Add water; bring to a boil over high heat. Add potatoes, bay leaves and tarragon; return to a boil. Reduce heat; cover and simmer 20 minutes or until potatoes are tender. Remove from heat.*

3. *Stir in navy beans, bacon or ham, oil, liquid smoke, salt, if desired, and pepper. Remove and discard bay leaves; let stand 10 minutes before serving.*

Makes 6 servings

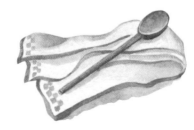

Winter Squash Soup

1 tablespoon butter
1 tablespoon minced shallot or onion
2 cloves garlic, minced
3 fresh thyme sprigs
1 pinch dried rosemary
2 packages (10 ounces each) frozen winter (butternut) squash,
    thawed
1 cup reduced-sodium chicken broth
3 tablespoons milk
    Sour cream (optional)

1. Melt butter in medium saucepan over medium heat. Add shallot, garlic, thyme and rosemary; cook and stir 2 to 3 minutes or until shallot is tender. Add squash and chicken broth; bring to a boil. Add milk; stir until blended.

2. Remove thyme sprigs from soup. Transfer soup to blender or food processor; blend until smooth. (Add additional liquid to make soup thinner, if desired.) Top with dollop of sour cream.   *Makes 4 servings*

Hearty Mushroom and Barley Soup

    9 cups chicken broth
    1 package (16 ounces) sliced fresh button mushrooms
    1 large onion, chopped
    2 carrots, chopped
    2 stalks celery, chopped
    $\frac{1}{2}$ cup uncooked pearled barley
    $\frac{1}{2}$ ounce dried porcini mushrooms
    3 cloves garlic, minced
    1 teaspoon salt
    $\frac{1}{2}$ teaspoon dried thyme
    $\frac{1}{2}$ teaspoon black pepper

Slow Cooker Directions

Combine all ingredients in 5-quart slow cooker; stir until well blended. Cover; cook on LOW 4 to 6 hours. Makes 8 to 10 servings

Variation: *For even more flavor, add a beef or ham bone to the slow cooker along with the rest of the ingredients.*

Cook Time: *4 to 6 hours*

Two-Cheese Potato and Cauliflower Soup

1 tablespoon butter
1 cup chopped onion
2 garlic cloves, minced
5 cups whole milk
1 pound Yukon gold potatoes (peeled or unpeeled), diced
1 pound cauliflower florets
1½ teaspoons salt
⅛ teaspoon ground red pepper
1½ cups shredded sharp Cheddar cheese
⅓ cup crumbled blue cheese

1. Melt butter in saucepan over medium-high heat. Add onion; cook and stir 4 minutes or until translucent. Add garlic; cook and stir 15 seconds. Add milk, potatoes, cauliflower, salt and red pepper; bring to a boil. Reduce heat; cover tightly and simmer 15 minutes or until potatoes are tender. Cool slightly.

2. Working in batches, puree soup in blender or food processor until smooth. Return to saucepan over medium heat. Cook 2 to 3 minutes or until heated through. Remove from heat; add cheeses. Stir until melted.

Makes 4 to 6 servings

SIDE DISHES

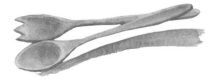

❧ ❧ ❧ ❧ ❧ ❧ ❧ ❧ ❧

Carrie's Sweet Potato Casserole

Topping (recipe follows)
3 pounds sweet potatoes, cooked and peeled*
$^1/_2$ cup (1 stick) butter, softened
$^1/_2$ cup granulated sugar
$^1/_2$ cup evaporated milk
2 eggs
1 teaspoon vanilla
1 cup chopped pecans

*For faster preparation, substitute canned sweet potatoes.

1. Preheat oven to 350°F. Grease 8 (6-ounce) ovenproof ramekins or 13×9-inch baking dish. Prepare Topping; set aside.

2. Mash sweet potatoes and butter in large bowl. Beat with electric mixer at medium speed until light and fluffy.

3. Add granulated sugar, evaporated milk, eggs and vanilla, beating after each addition. Spread evenly in prepared ramekins. Spoon Topping over potatoes; sprinkle with pecans.

4. Bake 20 to 25 minutes or until set.   Makes 8 to 12 servings

Topping: Combine 1 cup packed brown sugar, $^1/_2$ cup all-purpose flour and $^1/_3$ cup melted butter in medium bowl; mix well.

Bacon and Maple Grits Puff

8 slices bacon
2 cups milk
1 1/4 cups water
1 cup uncooked quick-cooking grits
1/2 teaspoon salt
1/2 cup pure maple syrup
4 eggs

1. Preheat oven to 350°F. Grease 1 1/2-quart soufflé dish or round casserole; set aside.

2. Cook bacon in large skillet over medium-high heat about 7 minutes or until crisp. Drain bacon on paper towels; set aside. Reserve 2 tablespoons bacon drippings.

3. Combine milk, water, grits and salt in medium saucepan. Bring to a boil over medium heat, stirring frequently. Reduce heat; simmer 2 to 3 minutes or until mixture thickens, stirring constantly. Remove from heat; stir in syrup and reserved 2 tablespoons bacon drippings.

4. Crumble bacon; reserve 1/4 cup for garnish. Stir remaining crumbled bacon into grits mixture.

5. Beat eggs in medium bowl with electric mixer at high speed until thick and pale. Stir spoonful of grits mixture into eggs until well blended. Fold egg mixture into remaining grits mixture until blended. Spoon grits mixture into prepared casserole.

6. Bake 1 hour 20 minutes or until knife inserted into center comes out clean. Top with reserved 1/4 cup bacon. Serve immediately.

Makes 6 to 8 servings

Note: Puff will fall slightly after being removed from oven.

Chunky Applesauce

10 tart apples (about 3 pounds), peeled, cored and chopped
$^3/_4$ cup packed light brown sugar
$^1/_2$ cup apple juice or apple cider
$1^1/_2$ teaspoons ground cinnamon
$^1/_8$ teaspoon salt
$^1/_8$ teaspoon ground nutmeg

1. Combine apples, brown sugar, apple juice, cinnamon, salt and nutmeg in large heavy saucepan; cover. Cook over medium-low heat 40 to 45 minutes or until apples are tender, stirring occasionally. Remove saucepan from heat. Cool completely.

2. Store in airtight container in refrigerator up to 1 month.

Makes about 5 $^1/_2$ cups

Country Green Beans with Ham

2 teaspoons olive oil
$^1/_4$ cup finely chopped onion
1 clove garlic, minced
1 pound fresh green beans
1 cup chopped fresh tomatoes
6 slices (2 ounces) thinly sliced smoked ham
1 tablespoon chopped fresh marjoram
2 teaspoons chopped fresh basil
$^1/_8$ teaspoon black pepper
$^1/_4$ cup herbed croutons

1. Heat oil in medium saucepan over medium heat. Add onion and garlic; cook and stir about 4 minutes or until onion is tender.

2. Reduce heat to low. Add green beans, tomatoes, ham, marjoram, basil and pepper. Cook about 10 minutes, stirring occasionally, until liquid is evaporated.

3. Transfer mixture to serving dish. Top with croutons.

Makes 4 servings

Festive Cranberry Mold

   $^1/_2$ cup water
   1 package (6 ounces) raspberry-flavored gelatin
   1 can (8 ounces) jellied cranberry sauce
$1^2/_3$ cups cranberry juice cocktail
   1 cup sliced bananas (optional)
   $^1/_2$ cup walnuts, toasted (optional)

1. *Bring water to a boil in medium saucepan over medium-high heat. Add gelatin and stir until dissolved. Fold in cranberry sauce. Reduce heat to medium; cook until sauce is melted. Stir in cranberry juice cocktail.*

2. *Refrigerate mixture until slightly thickened. Fold in banana slices and walnuts, if desired. Pour mixture into 4-cup mold; cover and refrigerate until gelatin is set.* *Makes 8 servings*

Apple-Stuffed Acorn Squash

   $^1/_4$ cup raisins
   2 acorn squash (about 4 inches in diameter)
   $^1/_4$ cup ($^1/_2$ stick) butter, melted, divided
   2 tablespoons sugar
   $^1/_4$ teaspoon cinnamon
   2 medium Fuji apples
   2 tablespoons butter

1. *Cover raisins with warm water and soak 20 minutes; drain. Meanwhile, preheat oven to 375°F. Cut acorn squash into quarters and remove seeds. Brush inside of each squash quarter with half of butter. Mix sugar and cinnamon. Sprinkle squash quarters with half of cinnamon mixture. Bake 10 minutes.*

2. *While baking, cut apples into quarters and remove cores. Chop apples into $^1/_2$-inch pieces. Combine remaining melted butter, apples, raisins and remaining cinnamon mixture in large bowl; mix well. Take squash from oven and top with equal amounts of apple mixture, making sure to scrape saucepan well. Return squash to oven and bake 30 to 35 minutes or until apples and squash are tender. Serve warm.* *Makes 8 servings*

Honeyed Beets

$1/4$ cup unsweetened apple juice
2 tablespoons cider vinegar
1 tablespoon honey
2 teaspoons cornstarch
2 cans (8 ounces each) sliced beets, drained
  Salt
  Black pepper

Combine apple juice, vinegar, honey and cornstarch in large nonstick saucepan. Cook, stirring occasionally, over medium heat until simmering. Stir in beets; season to taste with salt and pepper. Simmer 3 minutes.

Makes 4 servings

Glazed Parsnips and Carrots

1 pound parsnips (2 very large or 3 medium)
8 ounces baby carrots
1 tablespoon canola oil
  Salt and black pepper
$1/4$ cup orange juice
1 tablespoon unsalted butter
1 tablespoon honey
$1/8$ teaspoon ground ginger

1. Preheat oven to 425°F. Peel parsnips; cut into wedges the same size as baby carrots.

2. Spread vegetables in shallow roasting pan. Drizzle with oil and sprinkle with salt and pepper; toss to coat. Bake 30 to 35 minutes or until fork-tender.

3. Combine orange juice, butter, honey and ginger in large skillet. Add roasted vegetables; cook over high heat 1 to 2 minutes, stirring frequently, until sauce thickens and coats vegetables. Season with additional salt and pepper, if desired.

Makes 6 servings

Potatoes and Leeks au Gratin

5 tablespoons butter, divided
2 large leeks, sliced
2 tablespoons minced garlic
2 pounds baking potatoes, peeled (about 4 medium)
1 cup whipping cream
1 cup milk
3 eggs
2 teaspoons salt
$\frac{1}{4}$ teaspoon white pepper
2 to 3 slices dense day-old white bread,
    such as French or Italian
2 ounces grated Parmesan cheese
    Fresh herbs (optional)

1. Preheat oven to 375°F. Generously butter shallow 10-cup baking dish with 1 tablespoon butter; set aside.

2. Melt 2 tablespoons butter in large skillet over medium heat. Add leeks and garlic. Cook and stir 8 to 10 minutes or until leeks are softened. Remove from heat; set aside.

3. Cut potatoes crosswise into $\frac{1}{16}$-inch-thick slices. Layer half of potato slices in prepared baking dish. Top with half of leek mixture. Repeat layers with remaining potato slices and leek mixture. Whisk cream, milk, eggs, salt and white pepper in medium bowl until well blended; pour evenly over leek mixture.

4. To prepare bread crumbs, tear bread slices into 1-inch pieces and place in food processor or blender; process until fine crumbs form. Measure $\frac{3}{4}$ cup crumbs; place in small bowl. Stir in Parmesan cheese. Melt remaining 2 tablespoons butter. Add to crumb mixture; stir. Sprinkle crumb mixture evenly over vegetables in baking dish.

5. Bake 50 to 60 minutes or until top is golden and potatoes are tender. Let stand 5 to 10 minutes before serving. Garnish, if desired.

Makes 6 to 8 servings

Hush Puppy Batter

1$\frac{1}{2}$ cups yellow cornmeal
$\frac{1}{2}$ cup all-purpose flour
2 teaspoons baking powder
$\frac{1}{2}$ teaspoon salt
1 cup milk
1 small onion, minced
1 egg, lightly beaten

Combine cornmeal, flour, baking powder and salt in medium bowl. Add milk, onion and egg. Stir until well blended. Allow batter to stand 5 to 10 minutes before frying. See page 16 for frying instructions.

Makes about 24 hush puppies

Roasted Veggies with Nutmeg

8 ounces fresh cauliflower florets
1 medium onion, cut into $\frac{1}{2}$-inch wedges
3 medium carrots, peeled, cut into quarters lengthwise, then cut crosswise into 2-inch pieces
1 tablespoon vegetable oil
1 tablespoon sugar
$\frac{1}{4}$ teaspoon ground nutmeg
$\frac{1}{4}$ teaspoon salt
$\frac{1}{8}$ teaspoon black pepper

1. Preheat oven to 425°F. Line baking sheet with foil. Coat foil with nonstick cooking spray. Arrange cauliflower, onion and carrots on prepared sheet. Drizzle evenly with oil. Sprinkle evenly with sugar. Bake 6 minutes. Stir. Bake 6 to 9 minutes more or until lightly browned on edges.

2. Remove from oven. Sprinkle evenly with nutmeg, salt and pepper. Wrap vegetables in foil. Let stand 5 minutes before serving. *Makes 4 servings*

Cook's note: *Roasting brings out the natural sweetness and depth of flavor of the vegetables, so you may not need to add the sugar. Almost any vegetable can be roasted.*

Swiss-Style Vegetables

³/₄ cup cubed unpeeled red potato
2 cups broccoli florets
1 cup cauliflower florets
2 teaspoons butter
1 cup sliced mushrooms
1 tablespoon all-purpose flour
1 cup half-and-half
¹/₂ cup (2 ounces) shredded Swiss cheese
¹/₄ teaspoon salt
¹/₄ teaspoon black pepper
¹/₄ teaspoon hot pepper sauce (optional)
¹/₈ teaspoon ground nutmeg
¹/₄ cup grated Parmesan cheese

1. Place potato in medium saucepan; cover with cold water. Bring water to a boil. Reduce heat; cover and simmer 10 minutes. Add broccoli and cauliflower; cover and cook about 5 minutes or until all vegetables are tender. Drain; remove vegetables and set aside.

2. Melt butter in same pan over medium-low heat. Add mushrooms. Cook and stir 2 minutes. Stir in flour; cook 1 minute. Slowly stir in half-and-half; cook and stir until mixture thickens. Remove from heat. Add Swiss cheese, stirring until melted. Stir in salt, pepper, hot sauce, if desired, and nutmeg.

3. Preheat broiler. Spray small shallow casserole with nonstick cooking spray.

4. Arrange vegetables in single layer in prepared casserole. Spoon sauce mixture over vegetables; sprinkle with Parmesan cheese.

5. Place casserole under broiler 1 minute or until cheese melts and browns.

Makes 6 servings

Zucchini Delight

1 can (10 ³/₄ ounces) condensed tomato soup, undiluted
1 tablespoon lemon juice
1 teaspoon sugar
2 cloves garlic, minced
¹/₂ teaspoon salt
6 cups ¹/₂-inch zucchini slices (about 1¹/₂ pounds)
1 cup thinly sliced onion
1 cup coarsely chopped green bell pepper
1 cup sliced fresh mushrooms
2 tablespoons grated Parmesan cheese

Combine soup, lemon juice, sugar, garlic and salt in large saucepan. Add zucchini, onion, bell pepper and mushrooms; mix well. Bring to a boil; reduce heat. Cover and cook 20 to 25 minutes or until vegetables are crisp-tender, stirring occasionally. Sprinkle with cheese before serving.

Makes 6 servings

Green Peas with Red Bell Pepper Strips

2 cups frozen peas
2 tablespoons water
2 tablespoons butter
6 medium green onions, cut into ¹/₂-inch pieces
¹/₂ medium red bell pepper, cut into matchstick-size strips
¹/₄ teaspoon dried oregano
¹/₄ teaspoon salt

1. In medium microwave-safe bowl, combine peas and water. Cover; microwave on HIGH 2 minutes or until just heated through. Drain well.

2. Meanwhile, melt butter in large nonstick skillet over medium-high heat. Add green onions, bell pepper and oregano; cook and stir 4 minutes or until vegetables begin to brown on edges.

3. Add peas and salt; stir gently.

Makes 4 servings

BREADS

Buttermilk Corn Bread Loaf

1 1/2 cups all-purpose flour
1 cup yellow cornmeal
1/3 cup sugar
2 teaspoons baking powder
1 teaspoon salt
1/2 teaspoon baking soda
1/2 cup shortening
1 1/3 cups buttermilk*
2 eggs

*Or, substitute soured fresh milk. To sour milk, place 4 teaspoons lemon juice plus enough milk to equal 1 1/3 cups in 2-cup measure. Stir; let stand 5 minutes before using.

1. Preheat oven to 375°F. Grease 8 1/2 × 4 1/2-inch loaf pan; set aside.

2. Combine flour, cornmeal, sugar, baking powder, salt and baking soda in medium bowl. Cut in shortening with pastry blender or 2 knives until mixture resembles coarse crumbs.

3. Whisk together buttermilk and eggs in small bowl. Make a well in center of dry ingredients. Add buttermilk mixture; stir until mixture forms stiff batter. (Batter will be lumpy.) Turn into prepared pan; spread mixture evenly, removing any air bubbles.

4. Bake 50 to 55 minutes or until toothpick inserted in center comes out clean. Cool in pan on wire rack 10 minutes. Remove from pan; cool on rack 10 minutes. Serve warm.   *Makes 1 loaf*

Bran and Honey Rye Breadsticks

```
    1 package (¼ ounce) active dry yeast
    1 teaspoon sugar
 1½ cups warm water (110°F)
 3¾ cups all-purpose flour, divided
    1 tablespoon honey
    1 tablespoon vegetable oil
  ½ teaspoon salt
    1 cup rye flour
  ½ cup whole bran cereal
  ½ cup milk
```

1. *Combine yeast, sugar and warm water in large bowl. Let stand 5 minutes until bubbly. Add 1 cup all-purpose flour, honey, oil and salt. Beat with electric mixer at medium speed 3 minutes. Stir in rye flour, bran cereal and 2 cups all-purpose flour or enough to make moderately stiff dough.*

2. *Turn out onto lightly floured surface. Knead about 10 minutes, adding enough remaining flour to make a smooth and elastic dough. Place in greased bowl; turn over to grease surface. Cover with damp cloth; let rise in warm place 40 to 45 minutes or until doubled in bulk.*

3. *Spray 2 baking sheets with nonstick cooking spray. Punch dough down. Divide into 24 equal pieces on lightly floured surface. Roll each piece into an 8-inch rope. Place on prepared baking sheets. Cover and let rise in warm place 30 to 35 minutes or until doubled in bulk.*

4. *Preheat oven to 375°F. Brush breadsticks with milk. Bake 18 to 20 minutes or until breadsticks are golden brown. Remove from baking sheets. Cool on wire racks.*   *Makes 24 breadsticks*

Cheddar-Apple Bread

    2 cups all-purpose flour
    2 teaspoons baking powder
    1 teaspoon baking soda
 $^1/_4$ teaspoon salt
    1 cup sour cream
 $^1/_4$ cup milk
    1 cup packed light brown sugar
 $^1/_2$ cup (1 stick) butter, softened
    2 eggs
    1 teaspoon vanilla
 $1^1/_2$ cups diced dried apples
    1 cup (4 ounces) shredded Cheddar cheese

1. Preheat oven to 350°F. Spray 9×5-inch loaf pan with nonstick cooking spray; set aside.

2. Combine flour, baking powder, baking soda and salt in small bowl. Combine sour cream and milk in another small bowl. Beat brown sugar and butter in large bowl with electric mixer at medium speed until light and fluffy. Beat in eggs and vanilla until blended. Add flour mixture to butter mixture alternately with sour cream mixture, beginning and ending with flour mixture. Beat well after each addition. Stir in apples and cheese until blended. Spoon into prepared pan.

3. Bake 50 to 55 minutes or until toothpick inserted into center comes out clean. Cool in pan on wire rack 15 minutes. Remove from pan and cool completely on wire rack. Makes 12 servings

Tip: Brown sugar can become hard during storage, making it difficult to measure. To soften it, place the brown sugar in a microwavable bowl and microwave on HIGH 30 to 60 seconds or until softened.

Cheddar-Onion Loaf

1 cup water
1 package (¹/₄ ounce) active dry yeast
2 teaspoons sugar
2 cups all-purpose flour
4 tablespoons butter, softened and divided
2 eggs
¹/₄ teaspoon salt
1 cup whole wheat flour
1 large onion, finely chopped
4 ounces sharp Cheddar cheese, cut into ¹/₄-inch pieces
    (about 1 cup)
¹/₂ teaspoon poppy seeds

1. Heat water in small saucepan over low heat until temperature reaches 110°F. To proof yeast, sprinkle yeast and sugar over heated water in large bowl; stir until dissolved. Let stand 5 minutes or until mixture is bubbly. Add all-purpose flour, 2 tablespoons butter, eggs and salt. Beat with electric mixer at low speed until blended, scraping down side of bowl once. Increase speed to high; beat 10 minutes, scraping down side of bowl once. Stir in whole wheat flour until soft dough forms. Cover with plastic wrap; let rise in warm place 1 hour or until doubled in bulk.

2. Meanwhile, cook onion in remaining 2 tablespoons butter in small skillet over medium heat about 4 minutes or until tender. Remove from heat; cool.

3. Spray 9-inch pie plate with nonstick cooking spray. Sprinkle dough with cheese and half of onion, stir until evenly distributed. Turn into pie plate. Spoon remaining onion over dough; sprinkle with poppy seeds. Let rise in warm place, covered, about 1 hour or until doubled in bulk.

4. Preheat oven to 375°F. Uncover loaf. Bake 30 minutes or until loaf sounds hollow when tapped. Remove from pie plate. Cool on wire rack 30 minutes. Cut into 12 wedges before serving.   *Makes 12 servings*

Country Buttermilk Biscuits

2 cups all-purpose flour
1 tablespoon baking powder
2 teaspoons sugar
$\frac{1}{2}$ teaspoon salt
$\frac{1}{2}$ teaspoon baking soda
$\frac{1}{3}$ cup shortening
$\frac{2}{3}$ cup buttermilk*

Or substitute soured fresh milk. To sour milk, combine 2$\frac{1}{2}$ teaspoons lemon juice plus enough milk to equal $\frac{2}{3}$ cup. Stir; let stand 5 minutes before using.

1. Preheat oven to 450°F.

2. Combine flour, baking powder, sugar, salt and baking soda in medium bowl. Cut in shortening with pastry blender or 2 knives until mixture resembles coarse crumbs. Make a well in center of dry ingredients. Add buttermilk; stir until mixture forms soft dough that clings together and forms ball.

3. Turn out dough onto well-floured surface. Knead dough gently 10 to 12 times. Roll or pat dough to $\frac{1}{2}$-inch thickness. Cut dough with floured 2$\frac{1}{2}$-inch biscuit cutter.

4. Place cutouts 2 inches apart on ungreased baking sheet. Bake 8 to 10 minutes or until golden brown. Serve warm.   *Makes about 9 biscuits*

Drop Biscuits: Prepare Country Buttermilk Biscuits as directed in steps 1 and 2, except increase buttermilk to 1 cup. After adding buttermilk, stir batter with wooden spoon about 15 strokes. Do not knead. Drop dough by heaping tablespoonfuls 1 inch apart onto greased baking sheets. Bake as directed in step 4. Makes about 18 biscuits.

Sour Cream Dill Biscuits: Prepare Country Buttermilk Biscuits as directed in steps 1 and 2, except omit buttermilk. Combine $\frac{1}{2}$ cup sour cream, $\frac{1}{3}$ cup milk and 1 tablespoon chopped fresh dill or 1 teaspoon dried dill weed in small bowl until well blended. Stir into dry ingredients and continue as directed in steps 3 and 4. Makes about 9 biscuits.

Cranberry Cheesecake Muffins

1 package (3 ounces) cream cheese, softened
4 tablespoons sugar, divided
1 cup milk
¹/₃ cup vegetable oil
1 egg
1 package (about 15 ounces) cranberry quick bread mix

1. *Preheat oven to 400°F. Grease 12 muffin cups.*

2. *Beat cream cheese and 2 tablespoons sugar in small bowl until well blended; set aside. Beat milk, oil and egg in large bowl until blended. Stir in quick bread mix just until moistened.*

3. *Fill prepared muffin cups one-fourth full with batter. Drop 1 teaspoon cream cheese mixture into center of each cup. Spoon remaining batter over cream cheese mixture.*

4. *Sprinkle batter with remaining 2 tablespoons sugar. Bake 17 to 22 minutes or until golden brown. Cool 5 minutes. Remove from muffin cups to wire rack to cool.* *Makes 12 muffins*

Prep and Bake Time: *30 minutes*

Date Nut Bread

2 cups all-purpose flour
¹/₂ cup packed light brown sugar
1 tablespoon baking powder
¹/₂ teaspoon salt
¹/₄ cup (¹/₂ stick) cold butter
1 cup toasted chopped walnuts
1 cup chopped dates
1¹/₄ cups milk
1 egg
¹/₂ teaspoon grated lemon peel

1. Preheat oven to 375°F. Spray 9×5-inch loaf pan with nonstick cooking spray; set aside.

2. Combine flour, brown sugar, baking powder and salt in large bowl. Cut in butter with pastry blender or 2 knives until mixture resembles fine crumbs. Add walnuts and dates; stir until coated. Beat milk, egg and lemon peel in small bowl with fork. Add to flour mixture; stir just until moistened. Spread in prepared pan.

3. Bake 45 to 50 minutes or until toothpick inserted into center comes out clean. Cool in pan on wire rack 10 minutes. Remove from pan and cool completely on wire rack.   *Makes 12 servings*

Ham and Cheese Corn Muffins

1 package (about 8 ounces) corn muffin mix
$^1/_2$ cup chopped deli ham
$^1/_2$ cup (2 ounces) shredded Swiss cheese
$^1/_3$ cup milk
1 egg
1 tablespoon Dijon mustard

1. Preheat oven to 400°F. Line 9 standard (2$^3/_4$-inch) muffin cups with paper baking cups.

2. Combine muffin mix, ham and cheese in medium bowl. Beat milk, egg and mustard in medium bowl. Stir milk mixture into dry ingredients; mix just until moistened.

3. Spoon batter into prepared muffin cups, filling two-thirds full. Bake 18 to 20 minutes or until light golden brown.

4. Remove pan to wire rack; let stand 5 minutes. Serve warm.

Makes 9 muffins

Serving Suggestion: Serve these muffins with honey butter. To prepare, stir together equal amounts of honey and softened butter.

Prep and Bake Time: 30 minutes

Old-Fashioned Cake Doughnuts

3 3/4 cups all-purpose flour
1 tablespoon baking powder
1 teaspoon ground cinnamon
3/4 teaspoon salt
1/2 teaspoon ground nutmeg
3 eggs
3/4 cup granulated sugar
1 cup applesauce
2 tablespoons butter, melted
2 cups sifted powdered sugar
3 tablespoons milk
1/2 teaspoon vanilla
1 quart vegetable oil
Colored sprinkles (optional)

1. Combine flour, baking powder, cinnamon, salt and nutmeg in medium bowl. Beat eggs in large bowl with electric mixer at high speed until frothy. Gradually beat in granulated sugar at high speed 4 minutes until thick and pale yellow in color. Reduce speed to low; beat in applesauce and butter.

2. Beat in flour mixture until well blended. Divide dough into halves. Place each half on large piece of plastic wrap. Pat each half into 5-inch square; wrap in plastic wrap. Refrigerate 3 hours or until well chilled.

3. To prepare glaze, stir together powdered sugar, milk and vanilla in small bowl until smooth. Cover; set aside.

4. Roll out 1 dough half to 3/8-inch thickness. Cut dough with floured 3-inch doughnut cutter; repeat with remaining dough. Reserve doughnut holes. Reroll scraps; cut dough again. Heat oil in Dutch oven over medium heat until deep-fry thermometer registers 375°F. Adjust heat as necessary to maintain temperature.

5. Cook doughnuts and holes in batches 2 minutes or until golden brown, turning often. Remove with slotted spoon; drain on paper towels. Spread glaze over warm doughnuts; decorate with sprinkles, if desired.

Makes 12 doughnuts and holes

Apple Butter Rolls

1 can (11 ounces) refrigerated breadstick dough
2 tablespoons apple butter
¹/₄ cup sifted powdered sugar
1 to 1¹/₂ teaspoons fresh-squeezed orange juice
¹/₄ teaspoon fresh grated orange peel (optional)

1. *Preheat oven to 350°F. Lightly coat baking sheet with nonstick cooking spray; set aside.*

2. *Unroll breadstick dough. Separate along perforations into 12 pieces. Gently stretch each piece to 9 inches in length. Twist ends of each piece in opposite directions 3 to 4 times. Place twisted strip on prepared baking sheet; coil into snail shape. Tuck ends underneath. Repeat with remaining strips.*

3. *Use thumb to make small indentation in center of each breadstick coil. Spoon about ¹/₂ teaspoon apple butter into each indentation. Bake 11 to 13 minutes or until golden brown. Remove to wire rack; cool 10 minutes.*

4. *Meanwhile, stir together powdered sugar and enough orange juice in small bowl to make of drizzling consistency. Stir in orange peel, if desired. Drizzle over rolls. Serve warm.*   *Makes 12 servings*

Prep Time: *10 minutes*
Bake Time: *11 minutes*
Cool Time: *10 minutes*

Parmesan-Pepper Cloverleaf Rolls

3/4 cup plus 2 tablespoons grated Parmesan cheese, divided
1/2 teaspoon black pepper
1 loaf (1 pound) frozen bread dough, thawed

1. Knead 3/4 cup cheese and pepper into dough, adding cheese 2 to 3 tablespoons at a time, until evenly mixed. Divide dough into 12 equal pieces; shape into balls. Cover with plastic wrap; let rest 10 minutes.

2. Coat 12 standard (2½-inch) muffin cups and hands with nonstick cooking spray. Divide each ball of dough into 3 pieces. Roll each piece into small ball. Place 3 balls in each muffin cup. Cover rolls loosely with plastic wrap; let rise in warm place (85°F) about 30 minutes or until doubled.

3. Preheat oven to 350°F. Sprinkle rolls with remaining 2 tablespoons cheese. Bake 12 to 15 minutes or until golden brown.   Makes 12 servings

Prep Time: *15 minutes plus rising time*
Rise Time: *30 minutes*
Bake Time: *12 minutes*

Sour Cream and Onion Rolls

    1 cup chopped onion
    1 tablespoon butter
3¼ cups all-purpose flour
    1 package (¼ ounce) rapid-rise yeast
    1 tablespoon sugar
    1 teaspoon salt
    1 cup warm beer
 ½ cup sour cream
    2 tablespoons butter, melted

1. *In small skillet, cook onion in butter over medium-high heat for 3 to 4 minutes or until tender; set aside. In large mixing bowl, combine 2 cups flour, yeast, sugar and salt. Stir warm beer into flour mixture; add sour cream. Beat on high 2 minutes. Stir in ½ cup onions. Stir in enough remaining flour to make a soft dough. With greased hands, shape dough into 12 balls, smoothing tops. Place into greased 10-inch pie plate. Cover and let rise in warm place 20 minutes.*

2. *Preheat oven to 400°F. Brush tops with melted butter and sprinkle with remaining onions. Bake on lower rack in oven 25 to 30 minutes or until lightly browned.* Makes 1 dozen rolls

DESSERTS

Apple-Buttermilk Pie

2 medium Granny Smith apples
3 eggs
1$^1/_2$ cups sugar, divided
1 cup buttermilk
$^1/_3$ cup butter, melted
2 tablespoons all-purpose flour
1 tablespoon ground cinnamon, divided
2 teaspoons vanilla
2 teaspoons ground nutmeg, divided
1 (9-inch) unbaked pie shell

1. Preheat oven to 350°F. Peel and core apples; cut into small chunks. Place apples in bowl; cover with cold water and set aside.

2. Beat eggs in large bowl with electric mixer at medium speed until fluffy. Add all but 1 teaspoon sugar, buttermilk, butter, flour, 2 teaspoons cinnamon, vanilla and 1$^1/_2$ teaspoons nutmeg; beat at low speed until well blended. Drain apples thoroughly and place in unbaked pie shell.

3. Pour buttermilk mixture over apples. Combine remaining 1 teaspoon sugar, 1 teaspoon cinnamon and $^1/_2$ teaspoon nutmeg; sprinkle over top. Bake 50 to 60 minutes. Serve warm or at room temperature for the best flavor. Store in refrigerator. *Makes 1 (9-inch) pie*

Berry Cobbler

1 pint (2½ cups) fresh raspberries*
1 pint (2½ cups) fresh blueberries or strawberries,* sliced
2 tablespoons cornstarch
½ to ¾ cup sugar
1 cup all-purpose flour
1½ teaspoons baking powder
¼ teaspoon salt
⅓ cup milk
⅓ cup butter, melted
2 tablespoons thawed frozen apple juice concentrate
¼ teaspoon ground nutmeg

*One 16-ounce bag frozen raspberries and one 16-ounce bag frozen blueberries or strawberries can be substituted for fresh berries. Thaw berries, reserving juices. Increase cornstarch to 3 tablespoons.

1. Preheat oven to 375°F.

2. Combine berries and cornstarch in medium bowl; toss lightly to coat. Add sugar to taste; mix well. Spoon into 1½-quart or 8-inch square baking dish. Combine flour, baking powder and salt in medium bowl. Add milk, butter and juice concentrate; mix just until dry ingredients are moistened. Drop 6 heaping tablespoonfuls batter evenly over berries; sprinkle with nutmeg.

3. Bake 25 minutes or until topping is golden brown and fruit is bubbly. Cool on wire rack. Serve warm or at room temperature.

Makes 6 servings

Note: Cobblers are best served warm or at room temperature on the day they are made. Leftovers should be kept covered and refrigerated for up to two days. Reheat leftovers, covered, in a 350°F oven until warm.

Prep Time: 5 minutes
Bake Time: 25 minutes

Brownie Quilt Cake

1 package (18¼ ounces) brownie mix, plus ingredients
    to prepare mix
1 container (16 ounces) vanilla frosting
1 tube (4¼ ounces) chocolate decorator icing
    Assorted colored sugars
    Ribbon (optional)

1. Prepare brownie mix according to package directions and bake in 8-inch square baking pan. Cool in pan on wire rack 10 to 15 minutes. Run knife around edges to loosen. Remove from pan and invert brownie onto wire rack. Cool completely.

2. Transfer brownie to serving plate. Frost top with vanilla frosting. Place chocolate decorator icing in small resealable food storage bag and seal. With scissors, snip off one corner of bag. Gently squeeze bag to pipe quilt pattern on brownie. Fill in quilt pattern with colored sugars. Wrap edge with ribbon, if desired.   *Makes 8 servings*

Tip: For a large celebration, make four brownie quilts and place them together as an unusual and attention-getting edible centerpiece. Pipe a wide strip of chocolate frosting to "connect" the four quilts into one large quilt. Wrap all 4 quilts with one long ribbon.

Chilled Cherry Cheesecake

4 chocolate graham crackers, crushed (about 1 cup crumbs)
12 ounces cream cheese
8 ounces vanilla yogurt
$^1/_4$ cup sugar
1 teaspoon vanilla
1 envelope ($^1/_4$ ounce) unflavored gelatin
$^1/_4$ cup cold water
1 can (20 ounces) cherry pie filling

1. Sprinkle cracker crumbs onto bottom of 8-inch square baking pan. Beat cream cheese, yogurt, sugar and vanilla in medium bowl with electric mixer at medium speed until smooth and creamy.

2. Sprinkle gelatin into water in small microwavable bowl; let stand 2 minutes. Microwave on HIGH 40 seconds; stir and let stand 2 minutes or until gelatin is completely dissolved.

3. Gradually beat gelatin mixture into cream cheese mixture with electric mixer at low speed until well blended. Pour into prepared pan; refrigerate until firm. Spoon cherry filling onto cheesecake. Refrigerate until ready to serve. Makes 9 servings

Coconut Cream Pie

1 package (4-servings size) instant vanilla pudding mix
2³/₄ cups cold milk, divided
1 prepared (9-inch) graham cracker pie crust
1 envelope whipped topping mix
¹/₂ teaspoon vanilla
1 package (4 ounces) flaked coconut

1. Beat pudding mix and 1³/₄ cups milk in medium bowl with electric mixer until thick. Pour into pie crust and refrigerate 1 hour.

2. Beat whipped topping mix, vanilla and remaining 1 cup milk in large bowl with electric mixer at high speed 4 minutes until thick and fluffy; spread on pie. Sprinkle coconut evenly on pie. Refrigerate until ready to serve.   *Makes 8 servings*

Strawberry Dessert

2 cups graham cracker crumbs
¹/₄ cup granulated sugar
¹/₃ cup butter, melted
2 packages (8 ounces each) cream cheese, softened
1 cup powdered sugar
2 containers (6 ounces each) lemon-flavor yogurt
3 pints strawberries, sliced
1 container (12 ounces) frozen whipped topping, thawed

1. Combine cracker crumbs, granulated sugar and butter in medium bowl; mix well. Press into bottom of 13×9-inch baking dish.

2. Beat cream cheese and powdered sugar in medium bowl with electric mixer at medium speed 1 minute. Beat in yogurt until blended. Pour mixture over crust. Arrange strawberries on cream cheese mixture. Spread whipped topping over strawberries. Chill at least 4 hours or overnight before serving.   *Makes 9 to 12 servings*

Cookies and Cream Layered Dessert

1 cup cold milk
1 package (4-servings size) white chocolate instant pudding mix
1 package chocolate creme-filled sandwich cookies
1/4 cup butter, melted
2 packages (8 ounces each) cream cheese, softened
2 cups powdered sugar
1 container (8 ounces) frozen whipped topping, thawed
1 teaspoon vanilla
2 cups whipping cream

1. Combine milk and pudding mix in medium bowl; beat with wire whisk. (Pudding will be thick.) Set aside.

2. Finely crush cookies in resealable food storage bag with rolling pin or in blender. Combine 2 cups crushed cookies and butter in small bowl. Place on bottom of 2-quart trifle dish. Reserve remaining crushed cookies.

3. Beat cream cheese and powdered sugar 2 minutes in large bowl with electric mixer at medium speed until blended. Fold in pudding mixture, whipped topping and vanilla.

4. Beat whipping cream in large bowl with electric mixer at high speed until soft peaks form. Fold into cream cheese mixture.

5. Spoon 1/3 cream cheese mixture over crushed cookies. Sprinkle 1/3 of remaining cookie crumbs over cream cheese layer. Repeat layers twice using remaining cream cheese mixture and cookie crumbs. Refrigerate until ready to serve.   *Makes 12 servings*

Dad's Ginger Molasses Cookies

1 cup shortening
1 cup granulated sugar
1 tablespoon baking soda
2 teaspoons ground ginger
2 teaspoons ground cinnamon
1 teaspoon ground cloves
$^1/_2$ teaspoon salt
1 cup molasses
$^2/_3$ cup double-strength instant coffee*
1 egg
$4^3/_4$ cups all-purpose flour

*To prepare double-strength coffee, follow instructions for instant coffee but use twice the recommended amount of instant coffee granules.

1. Preheat oven to 350°F. Lightly grease cookie sheets.

2. Beat shortening and sugar in large bowl with electric mixer until creamy. Beat in baking soda, ginger, cinnamon, cloves and salt until well blended. Add molasses, coffee and egg, one at a time, beating well after each addition. Gradually add flour, beating on low speed just until blended.

3. Drop dough by rounded tablespoonfuls 2 inches apart on prepared cookie sheets. Bake 12 to 15 minutes or until cookies are set but not browned. Cool 1 minute on cookie sheets. Remove to wire racks; cool completely.   *Makes about 6 dozen cookies*

Lemon Cheesecake

Crust
35 vanilla wafers
³/₄ cup slivered almonds, toasted
¹/₃ cup sugar
¹/₄ cup (¹/₂ stick) butter, melted

Filling
3 packages (8 ounces each) cream cheese, softened
³/₄ cup sugar
4 eggs
¹/₃ cup whipping cream
¹/₄ cup lemon juice
1 tablespoon grated lemon peel
1 teaspoon vanilla

Topping
1 pint strawberries
2 tablespoons sugar

1. *Preheat oven to 375°F. For crust, combine wafers, almonds and ¹/₃ cup sugar in food processor; process until fine crumbs are formed. Combine crumb mixture and melted butter in medium bowl. Press mixture evenly onto bottom and 1 inch up side of 9-inch springform pan. Set aside.*

2. *For filling, beat cream cheese and ³/₄ cup sugar in large bowl with electric mixer at high speed 2 to 3 minutes or until fluffy. Add eggs one at a time, beating after each addition. Add whipping cream, lemon juice, lemon peel and vanilla; beat just until blended. Pour into prepared crust. Place springform pan on baking sheet. Bake 45 to 55 minutes or until set. Place on wire rack. Using knife or narrow metal spatula, loosen cheesecake from side of pan. Cool completely. Remove side of pan. Cover and refrigerate at least 10 hours or overnight.*

3. *For topping, hull and slice strawberries. Combine with sugar in medium bowl. Let stand 15 minutes. Serve over cheesecake.*   *Makes 16 servings*

Pfeffernüsse

3½ cups all-purpose flour
2 teaspoons baking powder
1½ teaspoons ground cinnamon
1 teaspoon ground ginger
½ teaspoon baking soda
½ teaspoon salt
½ teaspoon ground cloves
½ teaspoon ground cardamom
¼ teaspoon black pepper
1 cup (2 sticks) butter, softened
1 cup granulated sugar
¼ cup dark molasses
1 egg
Powdered sugar

1. Combine flour, baking powder, cinnamon, ginger, baking soda, salt, cloves, cardamom and pepper in large bowl.

2. Beat butter and sugar in large bowl with electric mixer at medium speed until light and fluffy. Beat in molasses and egg. Gradually add flour mixture. Beat at low speed until dough forms. Shape dough into disk; wrap in plastic wrap and refrigerate until firm, 30 minutes or up to 3 days.

3. Preheat oven to 350°F. Grease cookie sheets. Shape dough into 1-inch balls. Place 2 inches apart on prepared cookie sheets.

4. Bake 12 to 14 minutes or until golden brown. Remove cookies to wire racks; dust with sifted powdered sugar. Cool completely. Store tightly covered at room temperature or freeze up to 3 months.

Makes about 5 dozen cookies

Winter Fruit Compote

1 can (16 ounces) pitted dark sweet cherries in syrup, undrained
1 teaspoon cornstarch
1½ tablespoons honey
1 tablespoon almond-flavored liqueur or ½ teaspoon almond
   extract
2 ripe Bartlett or Comice pears, peeled, cored and cut into
   1-inch cubes
1 teaspoon chopped fresh mint
   Fresh mint sprigs (optional)

1. Drain cherries, reserving ¼ cup syrup. Combine reserved syrup and cornstarch in small bowl; mix until smooth. Add mixture to saucepan; bring to a boil over medium-high heat, stirring frequently. Reduce heat to simmer. As mixture begins to thicken, stir in honey and liqueur.

2. Stir in pears and cherries. Cook 2 minutes or until fruit is warm, stirring occasionally. Spoon into dessert dishes; sprinkle with fresh mint and garnish with mint sprigs, if desired. Serve warm or at room temperature.

Makes 4 servings

Chocolate Oatmeal Caramel Bars

1¼ cups uncooked old-fashioned oats
1 cup all-purpose flour
½ cup plus 2 tablespoons firmly packed brown sugar, divided
2 tablespoons unsweetened Dutch process cocoa powder*
¾ cup (1½ sticks) butter, melted
1 can (14 ounces) sweetened condensed milk
⅓ cup butter
½ cup chopped pecans
   Powdered sugar

*Natural unsweetened cocoa powder may be substituted. Dutch process cocoa powder has a stronger flavor and will bake a darker color.

1. Preheat oven to 350°F. Combine oats, flour, ½ cup brown sugar and cocoa in medium bowl. Add ¾ cup melted butter; mix until crumbly. Reserve 1 cup oat mixture for topping; press remaining oat mixture evenly into bottom of ungreased 8-inch square baking pan. Bake 15 minutes.

2. Combine sweetened condensed milk, ⅓ cup butter and remaining 2 tablespoons brown sugar in medium saucepan; cook and stir over medium heat about 10 minutes or until thick and pale in color.

3. Cool milk mixture slightly until thickened; spread evenly over baked crust. Let stand 5 minutes or until set. Add chopped pecans to reserved oat mixture; sprinkle over caramel layer, patting down gently.

4. Bake 20 to 22 minutes or until golden brown. Cool completely in pan on wire rack. Sprinkle with powdered sugar; cut into bars.   Makes 16 bars

Chewy Pecan-Gingersnap Triangles

20 gingersnap cookies, broken in half
$^{1}/_{2}$ cup (1 stick) butter, softened
$^{1}/_{4}$ cup granulated sugar
$^{1}/_{4}$ cup packed light brown sugar
1 egg, separated
$^{1}/_{2}$ teaspoon vanilla
$^{1}/_{8}$ teaspoon salt
1 teaspoon water
$1^{1}/_{2}$ cups chopped pecan pieces (6 ounces)

1. Preheat oven to 350°F. Line bottom and sides of 13×9-inch baking pan with foil, leaving 2-inch overhang. Spray foil with nonstick cooking spray.

2. Place gingersnap cookies in food processor; process until crumbs form. (Or, cookies may be placed in resealable food storage bag and crushed with rolling pin or meat mallet.)

3. Beat butter, granulated sugar, brown sugar, egg yolk and vanilla in medium bowl with electric mixer until well blended. Add cookie crumbs and salt; mix well. Lightly press crumb mixture into bottom of prepared pan to form thin crust.

4. Whisk egg white and water in small bowl. Brush egg white mixture evenly over crust; sprinkle evenly with pecans. Press pecans in lightly to adhere to crust.

5. Bake 20 minutes or until lightly browned. Cool completely in pan on wire rack. Use foil handles to remove bars from pan to cutting board. Cut into 3-inch squares; cut squares diagonally in half.   *Makes 24 triangles*